100 Unforgettable Moments in
Pro Golf

Bob Italia

ABDO & Daughters
Publishing

Published by Abdo & Daughters, 4940 Viking Drive, Suite 622,
Edina, Minnesota 55435.

Copyright © 1997 by Abdo Consulting Group, Inc., Pentagon Tower,
P.O. Box 36036, Minneapolis, Minnesota 55435 USA. International
copyrights reserved in all countries. No part of this book may be
reproduced in any form without written permission from the pub-
lisher.

Printed in the United States.

Cover Photo credits: Allsport
Interior Photo credits: Wide World Photo

Edited by Paul Joseph

Library of Congress Cataloging-in-Publication Data

Italia, Bob, 1955-
100 unforgettable moments in pro golf / Bob Italia.
    p. cm. — (100 unforgettable moments in sports)
Includes index.
Summary: Highlights some of the most memorable individual
accomplishments and professional matches in the history of golf.
ISBN 1-56239-694-3
1. Golf—History—Juvenile literature. [1. Golf—History.]
I. Title. II. Series Italia, Bob, 1955-   100 unforgettable
moments in sports.
GV963.I83 1996
796.352—dc20
                                    96-8142
                                     CIP
                                      AC

Contents

The Most Unforgettable Moment?

The game of golf has been around for centuries. Throughout its long history, there have been many great dramas played out on the countless courses all across the world. Who can forget the 1995 British Open playoff battle between John Daly and Costantino Rocca? Or Fred Couples' amazing bunker shot in the 1994 President's Cup that clinched the win for the U.S. team?

Some of professional golf's most unforgettable "moments" weren't moments at all. They took a year—or a lifetime—to accomplish, like Bobby Jones' Grand Slam in 1930, Jack Nicklaus' six Masters titles, or Sam Snead's 81-career tournament wins.

There is no one most unforgettable moment in professional golf. The following are listed in chronological order, not according to importance. That judgment must be left up to golf enthusiasts everywhere, whose passion for the game has made this sport legendary.

Opposite page:
Arnold Palmer tips his visor after dropping a birdie putt on the 7th hole during the final round of the National Open, 1960. It was his 6th birdie in 7 holes.

The 1913 U.S. Open

The 1913 U.S. Open changed the face of American golf. A 20-year-old man who lived across the street from The Country Club in Massachusetts beat two of Great Britain's best—and single-handedly launched golf into the national spotlight.

Francis Ouimet had spent his early years as a caddie, watching the best players at The Country Club. He would then go to a neighborhood cow pasture to imitate their swings on a three-hole course that he and his brother had built. As talented as he turned out to be, Ouimet had never battled players like Harry Vardon, winner of five British Opens, or Ted Ray, the longest hitter of his time.

In September 1913, Vardon led one group of Open players with a 36-hole score of 151. Ray led the others with 148. Ouimet carded a 152, then remained on the heels of the two British masters. He posted rounds of 77 and 74—only four strokes off co-leaders Vardon and Wilfrid Reid, and only two behind Ray.

In round three, another 74 left Ouimet in a tie with Vardon and Ray with only 18 holes remaining. Ouimet shot a disappointing 43 on the front nine of the final round. With six holes to go, he knew he needed two birdies at the par threes and pars at the four par fours to tie.

At the short 13th hole, Ouimet missed the green with his tee-shot. But then he chipped in for his two. He stayed on target with pars at both 14 and 15, but could manage only a par at the short 16th.

The 18th green at the Country Club in Massachusetts.

With two holes remaining, Ouimet needed a par and a birdie. His three came at the difficult 17th, where he knocked in a 20-footer. On the 18th hole, Ouimet missed the green with his approach shot. But then he chipped within five feet and sank his par putt.

The next day, Vardon was only a stroke behind Ouimet as they came to the 17th. But then his teeshot found a bunker and he bogeyed. Ouimet again made birdie, and at that point the championship was decided. Ouimet's round of 72 took the title by five strokes from Vardon and six from Ray.

With the win, Ouimet became the first American golf hero. Though never turning professional, he went on to become one of golf's top amateurs.

Bobby Jones' Grand Slam

In 1930, Bobby Jones came to the Merion Golf Club in Pennsylvania and played the U.S. Amateur. Having already won the British Open and the Amateur championships of the U.S. and Britain, this was the most important tournament of his career. Jones had the chance to win the Grand Slam of golf.

In those days, the first two rounds of the Amateur were 18 hole matches. The remaining three rounds went 36. Jones won both matches. He then beat Fay Coleman in the third round, and in the semifinal breezed by Jess Sweetser.

Gene Homans had defeated Lawson Little and Charlie Seaver to reach the finals. As the last obstacle to the Slam, Homans was nervous. He didn't par a hole until the 6th. After the morning 18, Jones was 7 ahead.

Both players reached the 29th hole in two. Jones hit his first putt close to the cup. To keep the match alive, Homans had to make his long putt. He rolled it carefully, but knew immediately it was off line. He then walked up to Jones to be the first to congratulate him on his historic feat. To this day, no one besides Jones has ever won golf's Grand Slam.

Bobby Jones is escorted to the club house at St. Andrews, Scotland, after winning the British Open, 1930.

Ben Hogan

In 1953, Ben Hogan came to Carnoustie, Scotland, with a chance at greatness. Earlier in the year, Hogan had won the Masters and U.S. Open. A win at Carnoustie would give him a triple crown—the greatest feat since Bobby Jones won the Grand Slam in 1930.

Hogan began with a 73 and then improved with each round on scores of 71-70-68. The final round was a course record that gave him a four-stroke victory. He later called this his most satisfying victory.

"Certainly others were pleasurable," he said, "but none of them gave me the feeling, the desire to perform, that gripped me in Scotland."

Hogan became only the third player in history to win the U.S. and British Opens in the same year (the others were Jones and Gene Sarazen) and the first to combine the two national championships with a win at the Masters. On his return to the United States, Hogan was given a ticker tape parade in New York City.

The victory also put Hogan in Sarazen's company as the only players to win all four of the Grand Slam events.

Opposite page: Ben Hogan is shown after chipping out of the rough grass during the 1953 British Open at Carnoustie, Scotland.

Palmer Marches In

Most golf historians agree that the greatest U.S. Open in history was in 1960 at Cherry Hills in Denver, Colorado. It was the last Open Ben Hogan threatened to win, the first Open Jack Nicklaus had a chance to win, and the only Open Arnold Palmer ever won.

The 29-year-old Palmer was at the top of his game, having won the Masters two months earlier. He was the favorite when he stepped to the first tee in round one. But he pushed his drive into a ditch that resulted in a double-bogey six.

From that point on, Palmer had to play catchup. A 72 left him four strokes behind Mike Souchak. After the second round, Palmer was eight behind Souchak. After the morning round on Saturday, Palmer was still seven back. Still, he refused to give up.

At the start of the final round, Palmer stepped to the tee of the 346-yard first hole and crushed a drive. The ball bounced through the rough and hopped onto the putting surface, 20 feet from the hole. Moments later, Palmer two-putted for a birdie that launched the most famous come-from-behind charge in a career known for come-from-behind charges. Palmer birdied six of the first seven holes and shot a 30 on the front nine and 35 on the back.

Palmer had two tough challengers chasing him—Ben Hogan and Jack Nicklaus. With six holes to go, the 20-year-old Nicklaus held a one-stroke lead. But he lacked the putting skills that would

one day make him great. Three putts from short range at 13 and 14 took him out of the race.

Hogan was tied with Palmer as he stood on the 17th fairway. He had less than 100 yards for this third shot to the par five. The flag was close to the front of the green, just a few yards from the edge of a stream. Hogan lofted the ball into the breeze, and the crowd began to roar in anticipation. But then the cheers suddenly turned to gasps as the ball landed a foot short of the green and rolled backward into the stream.

Hogan waded into the water and rolled up his right trouser leg to his knee. He blasted the ball onto the green, but then two-putted for a bogey that sent him to the final tee one stroke behind Palmer. Needing a birdie, Hogan drove into the lake and finished in a tie for ninth place, four strokes behind. Arnold Palmer had his greatest come-from-behind victory.

Arnold Palmer (L) and a young Jack Nicklaus after Palmer's victory in the U.S. Open, 1960.

Palmer vs. Nicklaus

In one of the classic confrontations in professional golf history, Arnold Palmer—the reigning king of the game—faced 22-year-old Jack Nicklaus in the 1962 U.S. Open at Oakmont.

Paired together in the first two rounds, Nicklaus immediately showed he would not be intimidated by Palmer as he birdied the first three holes. But then Palmer took command and moved to a share of the 36-hole lead. Nicklaus was three strokes behind. Palmer kept a share of the lead after 54 holes. Nicklaus was right behind him.

Arnie had troubles at the end of round three, missing three two-foot putts. But as the final 18 began, Nicklaus three-putted the first green.

Meanwhile, Palmer birdied two and four. By the 9th hole, he had a three-stroke lead. Facing a short par five, he tried to increase his lead with a birdie. Instead, he found the rough on his approach shot, then needed two shots to get out. After two putts, he had a bogey.

Up ahead, Nicklaus had picked up a birdie at 11 to move within one shot of the lead. When Palmer bogeyed 13, they were tied. Each player parred the remaining holes to force an 18-hole play-off.

Palmer was fully aware of Nicklaus' talent. Jack had won two U.S. Amateur Championships, and finished second to Palmer in the Open two years earlier at Cherry Hills.

Jack took the early lead in the playoff and was never behind. After six holes, Arnold fell four behind because of his putting problems. He rallied with birdies at 9, 11, and 12 to come within one stroke. One of his famous charging victories seemed at hand. But a bogey on the 13th knocked him from contention. Nicklaus won the playoff, 71 to 74.

This was Nicklaus' first victory as a professional. At age 22, he announced his intentions to the world: "I want to be the best golfer the world has ever seen."

That statement signaled the start of the greatest career in golf. Never in the history of athletic competition has a game been dominated as long as Nicklaus dominated professional golf. For more than two decades, whenever and wherever the world's best players gathered for a major championship, Jack was the man to beat.

Jack Nicklaus, age 22, grits his teeth as he misses his birdie putt in the 1962 U.S. Open.

Ken Venturi's U.S. Open Win

Few competitors in any sport have known the joy and the sorrow Ken Venturi experienced throughout his career. In 1956, he had a four-stroke lead at the Masters—and the chance to become the only amateur golfer ever to win that honored tournament. But Venturi collapsed with an 80 in the final round and lost.

Eight years later, Venturi was in the midst of a long slump that shook his confidence. But at the U.S. Open, he played 36 holes of courageous golf on a hot Saturday in June to become a champion.

In 1964, no one picked Venturi to win the Open. Winless in four years, Venturi had fallen to near-obscurity.

Venturi started the 1964 U.S. Open with an opening round of 72 that left him four behind Arnold Palmer. The next day, Tommy Jacobs took the halfway lead at 136 with Palmer one back. Venturi was six behind.

The final two rounds were played on the hottest, most humid days in the history of the Open. It was 100 degrees in the shade, and on one part of the course a thermometer read 115 degrees.

In the morning round, Venturi's game was sizzling. He hit his shots at the flag and sunk every makable putt on his way to a 30,

which tied an Open record. When Jacobs carded a 36, Venturi was tied for the lead.

Eventually the heat began to drain Venturi. He three-putted the 17th and 18th for a 66 that left him two shots behind Jacobs and two ahead of Palmer at the end of round three.

On the last day, Tommy Jacobs went four over on the first nine holes. Venturi played even par to take a two-stroke lead. When Jacobs bogeyed 10, Venturi was in control. It was his tournament to win or lose.

Ken Venturi strokes a putt in the 1964 U.S. Open.

Venturi added three more pars at 10, 11, and 12. When he sunk his 20-foot birdie putt at 13, Venturi held a four-stroke lead.

Three pars and a bogey later, Venturi wobbled down the final hill at 18. For the first time all day, Venturi smiled and waved his cap as the gallery cheered his gutty performance. When his final putt fell into the hole for a score of 278—at the time, the second lowest total in the history of the championship—Venturi dropped his putter and said with tears in his eyes, "My God, I've won the Open!"

The Changing of the Guard

The 1967 U.S. Open marked the day when Jack Nicklaus replaced Arnold Palmer as golf's reigning king.

Their rivalry began in 1960 when Palmer defeated Nicklaus in a tight race for the U.S. Open championship. Then in 1962, Nicklaus had won his first Open in a playoff over Palmer. In the years since that famous playoff duel, Nicklaus had won six major tournaments, Palmer three. After the 1967 Open at Baltusrol, Palmer would never win another major title. Nicklaus, however, would take another dozen—for a record total of 18.

Paired together in the third round, the two golf titans went at each other as if in match play, yet neither played well. Through the first 16 holes, neither had recorded a birdie. At one point Nicklaus said to Palmer, "Let's stop playing each other and play the course." Finally, Jack sank a 12-foot birdie putt at 17, then both players birdied the final hole. With 18 to go, Nicklaus and Palmer were tied, one shot behind the leader.

On Sunday, it was all Nicklaus. He birdied five holes on the front nine for a 31, shot a final round 65, and beat Palmer by four strokes.

The only real drama happened on the final hole. Coming to the 18th, Nicklaus needed a birdie to break Ben Hogan's 72-hole record. Jack took out his putter and rolled the ball into the cup for a birdie and the record 275. The new king had been crowned.

By 1967 Jack Nicklaus was the reigning leader on the tour.

Lee Trevino

The 1968 U.S. Open saw a slew of birdies and a winning score that tied the Open record. That score came from a Mexican-American raised by his grandfather in a shack without plumbing and heating. He was a player who quit school in the eighth grade and became a machine-gunner in the Marines. He taught himself golf in a pasture with a found club. He would eventually become the second-best player of his time, winning five major championships and several million dollars. His name was Lee Trevino.

Trevino shot 69-68 in the first two rounds, good enough for second place behind Bert Yancey, who tied the 36-hole Open record with 67-68. On Saturday, Yancey opened up a five-stroke lead by the 10th hole. But Trevino rolled in three birdies on the back nine as Yancey played one-over golf.

Trevino appeared at the first tee on Sunday wearing the outfit which he made famous during his first few years on Tour: a red shirt, black pants, red socks, black shoes, and a black baseball cap. When Yancey missed short par putts on three of the first five holes, Trevino took a one-stroke lead. Meanwhile, Jack Nicklaus made his move, birdieing 4 and 5 to pull within 3 shots.

Yancey missed another short one at 10 to fall two back. Then Trevino sank a 35-foot birdie putt at the 11th hole that gave him command of the tournament. He followed that with a second straight birdie at the 12th.

As he left the 12th green, Trevino looked at the scoreboard. He saw that he was five strokes ahead of Nicklaus. Trevino knew that if he played well, the 1968 U.S. Open Championship was his.

From 13 through 18, Trevino played even par, beating Nicklaus by four, Yancey by six. Even more, he tied Nicklaus's championship record with a four-foot par putt on the 72nd hole. With the win, Trevino completed a feat that had never been equaled in Open competition: he shot all four of his rounds in the 60s: 69-68-69-69. He also matched another Nicklaus feat—the U.S. Open was Trevino's first victory as a professional.

Lee Trevino tries to coax his putt in with some body English.

Johnny Miller Sets a Record

In the 1973 U.S. Open, 26-year-old Johnny Miller became a golf sensation by winning the tournament with a final-round 63—shattering the U.S. Open record.

During the mid-1970s, no one hit the greens more accurately than Johnny Miller.   In three years on the Tour, he had shot several low scores—including a 61 in the Phoenix Open. Not only could he hit the ball straight, he could also judge distances. Late in his career, Miller recalled: "For a while during my prime, I was disappointed every time a short iron shot failed to hit the stick."

A 76 in the third round had left Miller six strokes off the lead. But on the final day, he made his charge.

On the first hole, Miller hit a 3-iron five feet from the hole and made the putt for birdie. Then he almost knocked in a 9-iron shot at the second hole, leaving himself a 1-foot putt for a second birdie. On the 3rd hole, Miller hit a 5-iron shot 25 feet from the hole, then sank the putt for three birdies in a row.

On the 549-yard par five fourth hole, Miller's long drive allowed him to go for the green on his second shot. But the ball landed in a bunker. Miller's sand shot landed within six inches of the hole. Suddenly, he was four under par after four holes. Even more, Miller was only two behind the leaders who were just teeing off.

Miller suffered a 3-putt at the 8th hole, but birdied the 9th hole for a 9-hole score of 32—and one under par for the tournament.

Arnold Palmer, Julius Boros, and Tom Weiskopf were in the lead at four under par with nine holes remaining. But by this time, Miller was at the 15th hole tied for the lead, having birdied 11, 12, and 13. Miller knocked his 4-iron approach shot 10 feet from the hole, and rolled his putt in for his ninth birdie of the round. Miller parred the next two holes, then hit a long drive at 18. His 5-iron shot fell 18 feet above the hole, and his putt for a final round score of 62 lipped the cup.

Fourteen players still had to finish their rounds. Half had a chance to catch him. But an hour later, the last of the challengers failed to reach Miller's tournament score of 279. Johnny Miller was the champion. His 63 remains tied for the lowest round in U.S. Open history.

Johnny Miller throws a fist in the air after shooting a record 63 on the last round of the U.S. Open, 1973.

Watson vs. Nicklaus

The 1977 British Open duel between Tom Watson and Jack Nicklaus was the war to end all wars. Earlier that year, the two golf greats had faced each other at the Augusta National. Watson won despite Nicklaus' closing 66. But the drama of their match at Turnberry, Scotland, outshined the Masters—and nearly every other major championship in golf history.

Nicklaus and Watson opened with a 68-70 to move one behind the leader. Then in the third round the two giants separated themselves from the pack with a pair of 65s. With 18 holes left to play, Nicklaus and Watson were three strokes ahead of the field. Twenty-four hours later, third-place finisher, Hubert Green, was ten strokes behind.

On Sunday, Nicklaus took an early three-stroke lead when he birdied two of the first four holes while Watson bogeyed one. But Watson birdied the 5th, 7th, and 8th to draw even. A bogey at 9 left him one behind Nicklaus, who shot a 33. When Jack sunk a 25-foot birdie putt at the 12th hole, he was two strokes ahead.

Never had Jack Nicklaus held a two-stroke lead with six holes to play in a major championship and failed to win. But Watson charged ahead with a combination of great shotmaking and luck that created four birdies.

At the 13th, Watson pitched his second shot within 12 feet and sank the putt. At the short 15th, he hit the shot of the day. After driving his tee shot into the rough 60 feet from the cup, Watson knocked the next shot in with his putter to tie Nicklaus.

Both players parred the 16th—and then Nicklaus sealed his own fate at the par five 17th.

Watson had reached the green in two shots. But Nicklaus left his second shot short of the green. He pitched to five feet and watched as Watson missed his eagle putt. Jack missed his short birdie putt while Watson made his. With one hole to play, Watson had a one-stroke lead.

Nicklaus never gave up. After he pushed his drive into deep rough—just inches from a bush—Nicklaus muscled the ball onto the green. Watson countered with a great 7-iron to within two feet of the cup. But Nicklaus answered Watson's shot by sinking his 30-foot birdie putt. That forced Watson to sink his short putt to win the tournament—which he did.

The two golf greats left that final green smiling broadly, Nicklaus with his arm around Watson's shoulders. For four days, they had played their hearts out. And everyone who had watched the match—either at home or on television—knew they had seen something special.

Tom Watson and his wife kiss the British Open trophy after his victory.

Seve Ballesteros Arrives

In 1979, Seve Ballesteros of Spain came to Lytham, England, for the British Open. He spent seven days learning as much as he could about the course. By the time the tournament started, he had played 126 practice holes. He felt he was ready.

But Ballesteros' opening 73 left him eight behind the leader. The next day, however, Ballesteros made his move. He shot a 65 that was capped by a great finish. Hale Irwin posted a second straight 68 to take the lead, but Ballesteros was only two shots behind.

On Saturday, the wind died down, but the rain came, making play difficult. Irwin and Ballesteros, playing together, each shot 75, but maintained their lead.

The next day, Ballesteros played one of the more dramatic rounds in Open history. He began with a birdie on the first hole, then made a number of great recoveries to shoot a 34. By the 10th hole, Ballesteros was one shot ahead of Irwin. When Irwin three-putted the 11th hole, he fell two strokes behind.

On the 13th, Ballesteros nearly drove the green. But the ball caught a bunker. He hit a poor sand shot to the fringe—then sunk a chip shot for a birdie. Irwin two-putted for par to fall three shots down. He remained there until the 16th hole.

Ballesteros hit a big drive, but it was 40 yards right of the fairway. The ball landed near a hospitality tent—underneath an illegally parked car.

Since the car was locked, it was declared an immovable obstruction. Ballesteros was allowed a free drop. He played a pitch over some bunkers to within 20 feet of the flag, then sunk his birdie putt. Irwin, who parred the hole, could only shake his head in amazement.

Ballesteros hit two more wide drives at 17 and 18. But he still recovered for par each time to finish with a round of 70, the lowest score among the top ten players. He had hit only one fairway with his driver, and had missed each of the last six. But his recovering ability rattled Irwin, who stumbled in with a 78.

As the two players approached the final green, Irwin pulled a handkerchief from his pocket and waved it in surrender. "I cannot believe anyone can drive as badly as that and still win an Open," he said later.

Ballesteros won by three strokes over Ben Crenshaw and Jack Nicklaus. At age 22, he became the youngest British Open winner since Willie Auchterlonie in 1893.

Jack is Back

An article appeared in the 1980 U.S. Open program that read "Jack Will Be Back." But experts had their doubts. Since 1975, Nicklaus had won only one major championship, the 1978 British Open. Even worse, he had fallen to 71st place on the 1979 PGA Tour money list. Prior to that year, he had never finished lower than fourth.

But Baltusrol Golf Club in Springfield, New Jersey, inspired him. In the opening round, Nicklaus came to the 18th hole in need of a birdie to better the 18-hole record of 63. After three great shots, Nicklaus left himself a four-footer for a 62. But he pushed the ball to the right. Still, his 63 tied his longtime friend Tom Weiskopf for the lead.

Nicklaus' main challenger for the rest of the tournament turned out to be Isao Aoki of Japan. Using only 50 putts over the first 36 holes, Aoki shot 136, two behind Nicklaus, who shot a 71. Nicklaus' 134 was also an Open record. On Saturday, Aoki's third straight round of 68 moved him into a tie with Nicklaus. On Sunday, it became a head-to-head battle.

After eight holes, Nicklaus was one shot ahead. Then Aoki bogeyed nine and the lead was two. That was the way it remained. Each time Aoki tried to make a move, Nicklaus answered him with his own great shot.

The most dramatic was at the 17th hole. After Aoki knocked his third shot to within five feet for a certain birdie, Nicklaus sunk

a 20-foot birdie putt for a four of his own. As the ball hit the hole, Jack raised his putter in the air, and grinned from ear to ear—a picture seen on the cover of many books and magazines.

At the 18th hole, both players broke the 72-hole record. Aoki hit a pitch shot that nearly went into the hole for an eagle. Nicklaus rolled in his birdie for the winning 272, three better than the record he had set in 1967. The electronic scoreboard on the 18th hole said it all: "Jack Is Back."

Jack Nicklaus returns to dominate the 1980 U.S. Open with an eight under par 272.

Watson Conquers Nicklaus

In 1982, the U.S. Open returned to Pebble Beach. By then, Jack Nicklaus had begun to share his PGA tour dominance with Tom Watson. Since his first tour victory in 1974, Watson had won over two dozen more—including two Masters and three British Opens. For four years in a row (1977-80), he had led the Tour money list and been named the PGA Player of the Year. But he had not won the event he wanted most: the U.S. Open. At Pebble Beach, he would duel Nicklaus and try once again.

After two rounds, however, neither Watson nor Nicklaus was at the top. But in the third round, Watson made his move. His 68 tied Bill Rogers for the lead. Nicklaus lurked three shots behind.

When Nicklaus began the final round with two fives, he appeared out of the race. But then he rolled in five straight birdies, pulling ahead of Watson and catching Rogers.

Suddenly, all three players felt the pressure. Rogers began a string of mistakes on his way to a round of 74 and a tie for third. Nicklaus missed the green at the 8th hole and bogeyed, while Watson missed a two-foot par putt at the 7th. With nine holes to go, Nicklaus and Watson were tied.

The back nine drama was golf at its best. After hitting his second shot to the edge of a cliff at 10, Watson sank a 20-foot putt to save par. Nicklaus three-putted 11 to fall one shot back.

Watson birdied 11 on a 22-footer to go two shots up. But a bogey at 12 cut his lead in half.

Walking to his drive at 13, Watson heard a roar up ahead. Nicklaus had birdied 15 to tie for first. Watson parred the 13th, then rolled in a 40-foot birdie putt at 14 to regain the lead. Nicklaus finished the round with three pars. If Watson could do the same, he would win.

But at 16, Watson hit his teeshot into a deep right-hand bunker. With no shot to the green, he pitched sideways, got on the green in three, and two-putted for a bogey. Now he was tied with Nicklaus.

Watson's teeshot at 17 landed in the heavy rough a few feet from the green. Then he played one of the most famous shots in Open history. The ball popped out of the rough and into the hole for a birdie—and

Tom Watson hits out of the sand at the 1982 U.S Open.

a one shot lead. At the 18th green, Watson rolled in a 20-footer for birdie and a two-stroke victory. Once again, he had beaten Nicklaus—but this time for the U.S. Open.

Larry Nelson Stuns Watson

Halfway through the 1983 U.S. Open, defending champion Tom Watson had a share of the lead with Seve Ballesteros. It looked as though another battle of the titans in the tradition of Hogan/ Snead and Nicklaus/Palmer was about to take place.

But one other player had entered the picture. In the third round, Larry Nelson had birdied 7 of his last 11 holes for a 65 that had put him one back of Watson and Ballesteros.

In the final round, Watson birdied six of the first nine holes to card a 31 that left Ballesteros five strokes behind. But Nelson kept pace, shooting a 33 and keeping him three shots behind Watson with nine holes remaining.

Watson had trouble at the beginning of the back nine. He bogeyed the 10th and 12th holes as Nelson caught him with a birdie at 14—set up by pitch shot that landed a foot from the hole.

They remained tied for one more hole, and then a storm struck, suspending play until ten o'clock the next morning. Watson faced a 35-footer for birdie at the 15th. Nelson was at the tee of the par-three 16th. No one else had a chance to win.

On Monday, Watson narrowly missed his birdie putt. Nelson hit the green, but was over 60 feet from the hole. Incredibly, he sank the putt to take the lead. Nelson parred 17 but three-putted 18 to finish the tournament at 280, four under par.

Watson parred the 16th. But at 17, he missed the green with his approach shot, chipped to within five feet, and then missed the putt to fall to three under par. He needed a birdie at 18, but didn't get it.

Nelson's last two rounds were 65-67—the lowest final 36 holes in U.S. Open history. Not bad for a man who did not take up golf until 1969— after he had returned from the Vietnam War at age 21.

Larry Nelson waves to the gallery after a birdie on the seventh hole of the Oakmont Country Club during the final round of the 1983 U.S. Open.

Fuzzy and the Shark

In the first round of the 1984 U.S. Open, only two men bettered par—Fuzzy Zoeller and Greg Norman. They led the field by five strokes.

Halfway through the tournament, however, Hale Irwin took the lead, with Zoeller one shot behind, and Norman two. Irwin and Zoeller played together in the final round, and they quickly went in different directions. Irwin shot a 40 on the front nine, Zoeller a 32. Norman carded a 34 and was three shots behind.

It stayed that way after 13 holes as Zoeller was cruising. But at the par-four 14th hole, Norman rolled in a 20-foot birdie putt. Zoeller's tee shot found deep rough and he bogeyed the hole. Suddenly his lead was cut to one stroke.

Pars at 15 and 16 kept the lead at one with two holes remaining. But then Zoeller bogeyed 17 to fall into a tie with Norman. A pair of pars at 18 sent the tournament into an 18-hole playoff on Monday.

The playoff was expected to go down to the final hole. But when Zoeller rolled in a long birdie putt at the 2nd hole, he took a three-stroke lead on Norman, who recorded a double-bogey. Zoeller never looked back. By the 16th hole, Zoeller's lead had ballooned to nine strokes. Norman pulled out a white towel and waved his surrender as the two golfers approached the 18th green. The final score was Zoeller 67, Norman 75. Fuzzy Zoeller had won his first major tournament.

Opposite page: Greg Norman (right) congratulates Fuzzy Zoeller on his victory in the 1984 U.S. Open.

Ray Floyd Rises Again

Near the end of the first round of the 1986 U.S. Open, eight men were tied for the lead at one over par: Greg Norman, Hal Sutton, Lee Trevino, Bob Tway, Mark McCumber, Lanny Wadkins, Chip Beck, and Payne Stewart. Norman and Sutton had completed 7 holes, Wadkins had finished 16, and the rest were in between.

None of them would win. As the leaders began to falter, one man began to rise: Raymond Floyd.

No one had picked Floyd to win. Despite his good overall record that included two victories in the PGA Championship and a Masters title, Floyd had never been a strong contender in the U.S. Open. His best finish in 21 tries was a tie for sixth place. Even worse, just a week earlier at the Westchester Classic, Floyd had the lead going into the final round. But then he struggled to a 77 and lost the tournament.

During the three-hour drive to Southampton, Maria Floyd gave her husband a pep talk—and then he attacked the course with a new attitude. Floyd's 6-iron approach to the 13th stopped four feet from the hole. He rolled the putt in for a birdie. When Payne Stewart bogeyed the hole, they were tied for the lead. Then came the turning point at the par five 16th hole.

Floyd hit an 8-iron that stopped eight feet away. He sunk the putt for a birdie. Stewart struggled and bogeyed the hole. Suddenly, Floyd had a two-shot lead. With two closing pars, Floyd carded a 66 for the victory. At age 43, Floyd became the oldest man to win the U.S. Open.

Ray Floyd poses with his daughter, Christina, and the U.S. Open Championship trophy.

Norman's Revenge

Turnberry, Scotland, was the site of the 1986 British Open. Forty m.p.h. winds whipped the course on the first day. Only Ian Woosnam shot par of 70. During the second round, conditions improved slightly—allowing Greg Norman to play the round of his life.

Norman began the day with three straight birdies. Then he eagled the 7th, finishing the front nine with a 32. On the back nine, he birdied 10 and 11, hit the flagstick with his approach shot at 14 for another birdie, and then added a fourth at the 16th. Norman finished the second round with a 63—tying the one-round record for the British Open. Even more, Norman had seized a four-stroke lead.

The weather turned bad for the third round. Norman struggled with a 74, good for a one-stroke lead with 18 holes to go. His victory was hardly a sure thing. Norman had led the Masters and the U.S. Open after 54 holes, but did not win either one. Critics thought that Norman lacked what it takes to be a champion.

But the next day, Norman silenced his critics. He shot a final round of 69 to win the Championship by five strokes. Norman was the only player to match par for the 72 holes. He used the victory as a springboard, winning eight more tournaments that year and earning the position as the number-one ranked player in the world.

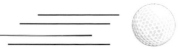

Greg Norman hits from the fairway in the British Open at Turnberry, Scotland, 1986.

Norman vs. Tway

In 1986, Greg Norman was on top of his game. He was the leading money winner on the Tour, and had won three events—including the British Open.

On the first day of the 1986 PGA Championship, Norman took the lead with a course-record 65. A pair of 68s in the second and third round took him to 202—one shy of the 54 hole PGA record. A third straight 68 would give him the tournament record.

But Bob Tway was having a good year as well. He was second on the money list, and he had won three times. Going into the final round, he was four shots behind Norman. It would be Tway vs. Norman the rest of the tournament.

A heavy rainstorm forced a one-day postponement. At the par-three 3rd hole, Norman hit his teeshot over the green and bogeyed while Tway sank a 12-foot putt for birdie. Just like that, the lead was only two strokes. But with nine holes to play, the lead returned to four.

At 11, Norman hit his teeshot into a sand-filled divot, then hit his second shot into a bunker and eventually double-bogeyed. The lead was back to two shots. Then Tway birdied 13, reducing the lead to one. When Norman bogeyed 14, they were tied with four holes to go. Through 15, 16, and 17, they remained even.

On the final hole, Tway drove into the rough, then missed his approach shot into the deep right-hand bunker. Norman hit his teeshot in the fairway, then knocked a wedge shot that struck the green, took a bounce toward the hole—then spun back 30 feet into the deep rough.

Tway's ball sat on top of the sand in the bunker. But he still faced a delicate shot that had to be hit perfectly if he wanted to save par.

Tway lofted the ball over the lip of the trap, struck the green—and rolled it into the center of the cup for a birdie. Tway jumped up and down with joy as Norman looked on in disbelief. He had planned to chip close to the hole and make a safe par. Now he had to sink the chip shot for a tie. Norman ran the ball straight at the flag, but the ball rolled by. Bob Tway had won his first major championship.

Bob Tway leaps into the air after sinking a birdie to win the PGA Championship.

Curtis Strange vs. Nick Faldo

In the 1988 U.S. Open, defending champion Scott Simpson took the halfway lead at 135 with Larry Mize only one shot behind. Curtis Strange was tied for third with Bob Gilder at 137 while Nick Faldo, Paul Azinger, and Fred Couples lurked a stroke further back. Twenty-four hours later, Strange had the lead by one over Faldo and Simpson.

Faldo began Sunday by parring the first 14 holes. Then he birdied 15 to tie Strange, with whom he was playing. But the tie lasted one hole as Faldo hit his teeshot into a bunker at the par-three 16th and made bogey. Strange rolled in a 25-foot putt for par.

With two holes to go, Strange had a one-stroke lead. At 17, Strange hit his approach shot 15 feet from the hole. But he misjudged the speed of his first putt and knocked it six feet past the hole. When he missed his next putt, he and Faldo were tied.

On the final hole, Strange plunked his approach into a deep bunker. But then he lobbed his next shot a foot below the hole and sank his par putt. When Faldo two-putted from 25 feet, a playoff was set for Monday.

In the playoff, Faldo made the first mistake, bogeying the 3rd hole. Strange took the lead—and was never behind all day. He clinched the victory on the 433-yard 13th, where Strange sank a

29-foot birdie putt while Faldo three-putted from 50 feet. That gave Strange a three-shot lead which he carried to 18. Strange hit the final green and two-putted for his par as Faldo bogeyed. For the day, Strange shot a 71 while Faldo ballooned to a 75.

Strange's victory was bittersweet. While fulfilling a dream, it also fulfilled a mission dedicated to his father. He was a golf professional who had started Strange in the game before dying of cancer at age 38. Strange went on to win four events on the U.S. Tour that year. He became the PGA Tour Player of the Year and set a new single-season money-winning record.

Curtis Strange hits out of the sand at the U.S. Open, 1988.

Nick Faldo Wins the British Open

Nick Faldo dominated the 1990 British Open. He scored a five-stroke victory and broke the previous St. Andrews 72-hole record by six strokes.

In the first round, Faldo hit a huge drive down the 18th fairway and nearly onto the green. Then he knocked his approach shot at the flag and into the hole for an eagle two. That gave him a round of 67, one behind co-leaders Michael Allen and Greg Norman.

The next day, Faldo battled Norman all day. Norman shot a 66 while Faldo carded a 65. Each player shared the lead at 12 under, 4 strokes ahead of the closest challengers. Golf fans hoped for a titanic weekend battle between the two top players in the world, but it never materialized.

In the third round, Norman struggled to a 76 while Faldo continued firing away at the Old Course, posting another 67 that put him at 199, 17 under par, for a new 54-hole Open record.

Faldo began the final round with a five-stroke lead. Only Payne Stewart got within two before fading at the end. The 1990 Masters Champion had won his second major of the year—and his fourth in as many years.

**England's Nick Faldo in action on the 2nd hole at the
British Open, 1990.**

Fred Couples and the President's Cup

The shot that won the first President's Cup for the United States in 1994 was one that would make the event famous.

The shot didn't look like much at first. Then it quickly found the right line, took a favorable bounce off the slope of the green, and rolled to within a foot of the hole.

It was hit by Fred Couples, one of America's most popular golfers. When Couples walked up to the 18th green, the crowd roared "Freddie, Freddie!" and "USA! USA!" A major golf event had just been born. Couples' birdie beat Nick Price by one stroke, providing the 17th and deciding point in the United States' 20-12 victory over the International team.

From a fairway bunker, Couples hit a right-to-left 9-iron shot that traveled 147 yards and rolled like a putt toward the hole. Price conceded the birdie to Couples—then nearly chipped in for birdie.

"Freddie's shot was a great one," said Price, the world's No. 1 player who didn't win a match in three days. "It would have been great if I could have made the chip shot, too. But the way it turned out, Freddie deserved to win the match."

Fred Couples tips his visor to the crowd after his shot on the 18th hole helped win the President's Cup.

Corey Pavin Wins a Major

At the 1995 U.S. Open, 25-m.p.h. wind gusts sent scores soaring. Corey Pavin was close to the lead all week. But a bogey five at the third hole of the final round dropped him five shots behind the leader, Tom Lehman.

Then Pavin started to regroup. He carded a string of five pars, then dropped a six-foot birdie putt at the ninth, followed by a 12-foot birdie at the 12th.

That's when the leaders started faltering. Bob Tway and Phil Mickelson failed to par the 16th. Davis Love III fell back with a bogey at 13 and a double-bogey 6 at the 18th. Lehman double-bogeyed the 16th and bowed out.

Finally, it was Greg Norman's turn. Making only one birdie over his final 36 holes, he fell to one-under at 15—but still had the lead.

On the 18th hole, Pavin hit the shot of a lifetime. From 228 yards out, the ball took a small bend and landed on the green, then rolled just five feet from the pin—sending up a roar Greg Norman heard two holes away.

Pavin raced down the 18th fairway and he leaped with joy, trying to sneak a peek at his shot. He then knelt in the fairway and said a prayer, giving thanks for the shot that set up his final birdie.

When Norman failed to hold the lead, Pavin—who had come from three shots behind—had won his first U.S. Open, and his first major championship.

Corey Pavin waves to the crowd after the final round of the 1995 U.S. Open.

John Daly
Comes of Age

In 1991, John Daly blasted onto the PGA scene with his stunning, overpowering victory at the PGA Championship in Carmel, Indiana. An unknown player at the time, Daly didn't even make the cut for the tournament. He drove back to his home in Memphis, Tennessee—only to learn that he had made it after all because another player had to drop out. Daly drove all night, played the next day—and became an overnight sensation with his titanic drives. Not only did he win the championship, Daly ended the year with a record for rookie money winnings and the Rookie of the Year title.

But since that time, Daly had struggled. Prone to lapses in concentration, he would often give up during tournaments after his poor scoring left him well off the leaderboard. Personal problems also kept him from realizing his true potential.

So when John Daly entered the 1995 British Open, no one paid much attention to him. After all, in 1993 and 1994, Daly had finished dead last in each British Open tournament. No one could have predicted the wildest end to the craziest British Open the Old Course at St. Andrews had ever seen.

John Daly won the tournament in a four-hole playoff over Costantino Rocca of Italy. He did it in a rare, un-Daly-like fashion—by remaining patient when those around him could not. He

Italy's Costantino Rocca celebrates after sinking a seemingly impossible 65-foot putt for birdie, sending him into a playoff against American John Daly in the British Open.

also did it by hitting impossible shots—and, more impressively, by refusing to quit.

Daly began the final round four strokes behind the leader, Michael Campbell. Then he slugged his way to a three-stroke lead by the 13th hole. But bogeys at the 16th and 17th holes cut the lead to one stroke.

That's when the golf gods seemed to test Daly. Rocca needed a birdie on the final hole to tie the match. He hit a long drive that nearly reached the green. All he needed to do was chip close to the hole to set up his birdie putt. But then something unexpected happened—Rocca flubbed the chip. Now he had to sink a seemingly unmakable 65-foot putt for birdie.

Daly was watching the drama unfold with his wife at his side, anticipating his second major victory. Then something even more incredible happened—Rocca knocked in his putt! Daly looked on in disbelief. Few thought he could recover from the shock in time to defeat Rocca in the upcoming playoff.

"When Costantino made that putt, my spirits kind of sunk," Daly admitted. "I was hoping it was over. But it wasn't."

John Daly at the 1995 British Open.

Daly's face suddenly hardened with determination. He and his caddie headed for the practice putting green next to the first tee, walking right past Rocca.

"Nobody would have dreamed Rocca would make that putt," Daly said. "And when he did, I just had to dig deep down inside. When it went in, I was that close to having a heart attack."

Daly was filled with determination when he stepped to the tee in the playoff. It ended quickly. Daly parred the first hole while Rocca bogeyed it. Then Daly rolled in a 25-foot birdie on the second hole. Rocca parred it from 10 feet away.

On the next hole, Rocca drove his ball into the Road Hole bunker. When it took him two shots to get out, the tournament was over. Daly hit a 9-iron into the middle of the green and parred the hole while Rocca made triple-bogey seven. Daly stepped to the final tee with a five-stroke lead.

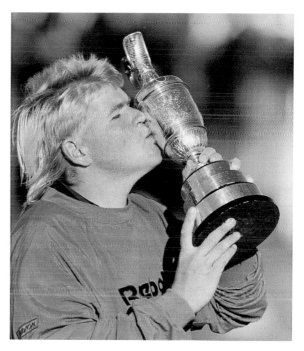

John Daly kisses the trophy after winning the British Open.

With the victory—his second major tournament win—Daly finally showed he could stay focused on his game when the world around him seemed to be crumbling.

The Masters Disaster

Nick Faldo won the 1996 Masters after some solid play. But the big news was Greg Norman's inability to tame his nerves and the difficult Augusta National Golf Course, as he let one of the biggest leads in Masters history slip away.

Norman let his six-stroke lead shrink to two strokes at the end of the first nine holes of the final round. Then he bogeyed the 11th, and double bogeyed the par three 12th. Suddenly, Norman was in second place—two strokes behind Faldo.

On the back nine, Faldo played "Amen Corner"—holes 11, 12, and 13—with two pars and a two-putt birdie. Though he seemed unbeatable during the first three rounds, Norman lost the form that helped him forge his big lead.

As bad as Norman's afternoon had been, it would hit rock bottom at the par three 16th hole. Norman pull-hooked his tee shot into the pond that bordered the 16th green. A double bogey left him at minus seven—four strokes behind Faldo.

Both players parred the 17th and Faldo birdied the 18th. But the tournament was already over. The gallery of normally loud Norman supporters was reduced to a silent mob of polite applauders, stunned by Norman's amazing fall.

Faldo hugged Norman when it was over and whispered to the Shark, "I don't know what to say. I just want to hug you. You're a great player and the game needs you."

Collapse, failure, choke. These were the words the press used to describe Norman's final round. But no one was more disap-

Greg Norman agonizes over an errant tee shot on the 16th hole.

pointed than Norman, a player who has geared his whole career toward winning the Masters. Norman seemed to have the tournament in his back pocket, but could not survive the pressure of leading the world's most honored tournament.

"I honestly and genuinely feel sorry for Greg and what he's going through," said Faldo, who added a third green jacket to a major-championship collection that also includes three British Opens. "I hope I'm remembered for shooting 67 on the last day and storming through. But obviously it's going to be remembered for what happened to Greg."

It was Norman's tournament to win or lose. He lost.

More Unforgettable Moments

1862—Tom Morris, Sr., wins the British Open by 13 strokes.

1867—Tom Morris, Sr., wins his fourth British Open.

1868—Seventeen-year-old Tom Morris, Jr., becomes the youngest player to win the British Open, beating his father, runner-up, Tom Morris, Sr.

1872—Tom Morris, Jr., wins his fourth consecutive British Open.

1899—Willie Smith wins the U.S. Open by 11 strokes.

1905—Willie Anderson wins his fourth U.S. Open.

1911—Nineteen-year-old John McDermott becomes the youngest player to win the U.S. Open.

1912—John McDermott wins his second-straight U.S. Open.

1912—Edward Ray wins the British Open wire-to-wire.

1914—Walter Hagen wins the U.S. Open wire-to-wire.

1914—Harry Vardon wins his sixth British Open.

Bobby Jones hits out of a sand trap at Winged Foot, 1929.

1921—Jim Barnes wins the U.S. Open by nine shots.

1922—Twenty-year-old Gene Sarazen becomes the youngest player to win the PGA Championship.

1925—Jim Barnes rallies from five shots down to win the British Open.

1927—Bobby Jones wins the British Open wire-to-wire.

1927—Walter Hagen wins his fifth PGA Championship.

1930—Bobby Jones wins his fourth U.S. Open and his second-straight U.S. Open.

1931—Tommy Armour rallies from five shots down to win the British Open.

1932—Gene Sarazen wins the British Open wire-to-wire.

1934—Henry Cotton wins the British Open wire-to-wire.

Tommy Armour and wife after winning the British Open, 1931.

1938—Ralph Guldahl wins his second-straight U.S. Open.

1940—Jimmy Demaret shoots a 30 on the back 9 in the first round of the Masters.

1941—Craig Wood wins the Masters wire-to-wire.

1948—Sam Snead records his sixth consecutive subpar round in the U.S. Open.

1950—Jimmy Demaret wins his third Masters.

1951—Ben Hogan wins his second-straight U.S. Open.

1953—Ben Hogan wins his fourth U.S. Open.

1954—Sam Snead wins his third Masters.

1955—Cary Middlecoff wins the Masters by seven strokes.

1956—Jack Burke, Jr. comes from eight shots back in the final round to win the Masters.

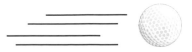

1960—Arnold Palmer wins the Masters wire-to-wire.

1960—Arnold Palmer rallies from seven strokes down on the final day to win the U.S. Open.

1964—Bobby Nichols shoots a 271 in the PGA Championship.

1966—Gene Littler shoots a 30 on the back 9 in the third round of the Masters.

1966—Jack Nicklaus wins his second straight Masters.

1967—Ben Hogan shoots a 30 on the back 9 in the third round of the Masters.

Johnny Miller just misses a 40-foot putt at the Masters.

1968—Forty-eight-year-old Julius Boros becomes the oldest player to win the PGA Championship.

1970—Miller Barber shoots a 30 on the back 9 in the fourth round of the Masters.

1970—Tony Jacklin wins the U.S. Open by seven shots.

1971—Jack Nicklaus wins the PGA Championship wire-to-wire.

1972—Jack Nicklaus wins the Masters wire-to-wire.

1972—George Burns records six consecutive birdies in the U.S. Open.

1973—Johnny Miller shoots a 63 in the fourth round of the U.S. Open.

1973—Tom Weiskopf wins the British Open wire-to-wire.

1974—Bruce Crampton records four eagles in the Masters.

1975—Johnny Miller shoots a 30 on the front 9 in the third round of the Masters; also sinks 6 consecutive birdies.

1975—Bruce Crampton shoots a 63 in the second round of the PGA Championship.

1976—Jerry Pate joins Jack Nicklaus and Lee Trevino as the only golfers to make the U.S. Open their first professional victory.

1976—Ray Floyd's 271 sets a Masters record; he also wins the tournament by 8 strokes.

1977—Hubert Green records 7 consecutive 3s in the U.S. Open.

1977—Mark Hayes shoots a 63 in the second round of the British Open.

1978—John Mahaffey rallies from seven shots down on the final day to win the PGA Championship.

1979—Jerry Pate shoots his sixth consecutive subpar round in the PGA Championship.

1980—Twenty-three-year-old Seve Ballesteros becomes the youngest player to win the Masters; also records 24 subpar holes in the same tournament.

1980—Jack Nicklaus shoots a 272 in the U.S. Open.

1980—Tom Weiskopf shoots a 63 in the first round of the U.S. Open.

1980—Isao Aoki shoots a 63 in the third round of the British Open.

1980—Jack Nicklaus wins the PGA Championship by seven shots.

1981—David Graham shoots a 273 in the U.S. Open.

1982—Ray Floyd shoots a 63 in the first round of the PGA Championship.

1982—Fred Couples shoots a 29 for 9 holes in the PGA Championship.

Gary Player hits out of the sand at the Masters.

1983—Sam Snead plays in his 44th consecutive Masters.

1983—Craig Stadler shoots a 63 in the first round of the British Open.

1983—Denis Durnian shoots a 28 for 9 holes in the British Open.

1983—Gibby Gilbert shoots a 29 for 9 holes in the PGA Championship.

1983—Hal Sutton wins the PGA Championship wire-to-wire.

1984—Gary Player shoots a 63 in the second round of the PGA Championship.

1985—Lee Trevino shoots his sixth consecutive subpar round in the PGA Championship.

1986—Nick Price shoots a third-round 63 in the Masters.

1986—Greg Norman shoots a 63 in the second round of the British Open.

The gallery watches Greg Norman chip to the green during the PGA Championship, 1986.

1987—Jodie Mudd records seven consecutive 3s in the Masters.

1988—Peter Jacobsen records seven consecutive 3s in the U.S. Open.

1990—Nick Faldo wins his second straight Masters.

1990—Hale Irwin wins his third U.S. Open.

1995—Ben Crenshaw wins the Masters one week after his lifelong teacher, Harvey Penick, dies following a long illness.

Index